A NEW WORLD OF DREAMS

IS BORN ON EACH

NEW CANVAS

THROUGH
# ANA'S EYES

ANA TZAREV GALLERY

24 W 57 STREET

NEW YORK

# ANA TZAREV

## ANA'S EYES

**Published by Accademia Publishing Limited**

©2009 Accademia Publishing Limited. All rights reserved.

All quotations by Ana Tzarev

Designed by Sabine Schoep

Cover photography by Brigitte Lacombe

Photography of artwork by John Riddy

Photography of Ana Tzarev by Sabine Schoep

Printed in Florence, Italy by Conti Tipocolor

ISBN 978-976-8214-17-1

Limited Edition of 10 000 copies in English

Paintings in this book courtesy of the Ana Tzarev Foundation

Right: Hanuman Triumphs over the Sea Monster, Oil on Linen, 2007, 195 x 195 cm (76,8 x 76,8 in)

Following Pages: Bida (detail), Oil on Linen, 1995, 61 x 50 cm (24,1 x 19,7 in)

# ANA TZAREV

SEE THE WORLD THROUGH ANA'S EYES

ALL TEXT AND QUOTATIONS BY ANA TZAREV

ACCADEMIA PUBLISHING LIMITED

ART AWAKENS

THE DREAM OF THE ARTIST

AND MAKES IT REAL

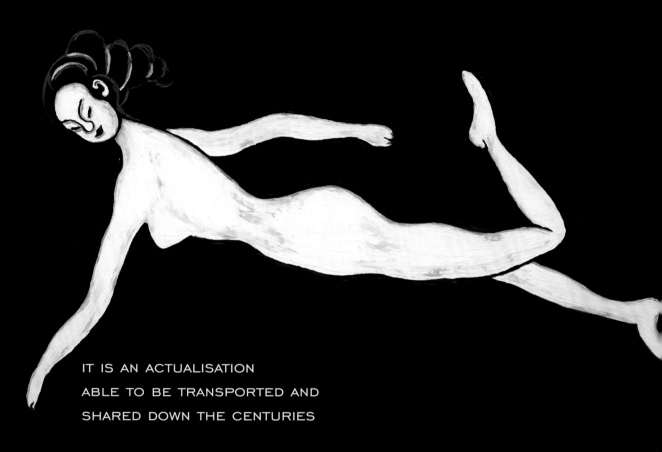

IT IS AN ACTUALISATION
ABLE TO BE TRANSPORTED AND
SHARED DOWN THE CENTURIES

IT IS A POSTCARD FROM THE ARTIST
TO FUTURE GENERATIONS AND FOR
THE SHARING OF THE GIFT WITH US ALL

**Star Catcher**
Oil on Linen, 2002, 130 x 162 cm (51,2 x 63,8 in)

16

DREAM AND DON'T LET ANYONE ASSASSINATE YOUR DREAMS

NURTURE THEM - THEY ARE YOUR CHILDREN

MAKE THEM BECOME REALITY, AND THAT

REALITY WILL BECOME

# YOU

Passion

Oil on Linen, 2002, 130 x 97 cm (51,2 x 38,2 in)

IMAGINATION IS THE SEED, WHICH,

WHEN PLANTED IN THE wOmb

OF THE MIND OF MAN

GIVES BIRTH TO A NEW WORLD

**Sunset Bathers**
Oil on Linen, 2003, 195 x 195 cm (76,8 x 76,8 in)

19

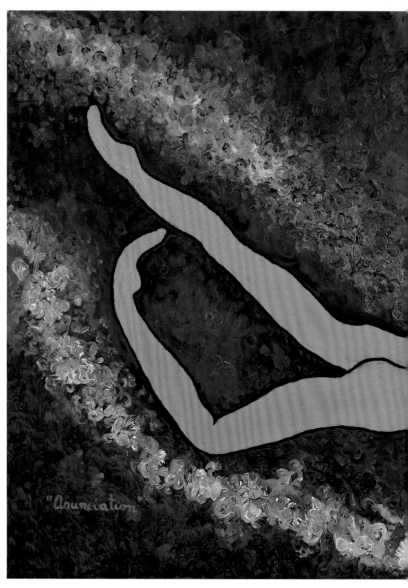

**Annunciation**
Oil on Linen, 2006, 200 x 400 cm (78,7 x 157,5 in)

THE GREATEST MAGIC YOU COMMAND IS

JUST ONE SECOND —

FOR EVERYTHING HAPPENS IN IT —

CONCEPTION AND DEATH AND

ALL LIFE IN-BETWEEN —

USE IT WISELY -

IT IS YOUR LIFE

**Moonlight Sonata**
Oil on Linen, 2002, 146 x 114 cm (57,5 x 44,9 in)

COLOURS ARE THE STRINGS OF THE

INSTRUMENT ON WHICH I COMPOSE MY WORLD

L**O**VERS

ARE

S**O**ULS

SPLIT BY BIRTH

AND MADE ONE

WHEN THE HAND

OF DESTINY

REUNITES THEM

**Embrace**
Oil on Linen, 2005, 146 x 114 cm (57,5 x 44,9 in)

31

**Love Songs**
Oil on Linen, 1999, 65 x 81 cm (25,6 x 31,9 in)

COLOUR IS THE MUSIC OF THE SIGHTED

LOOK FOR THE COLOUR AROUND YOU

AND YOU WILL HEAR THE SONG OF LIFE

**Blue Music**
Oil on Linen, 2002, 73 x 92 cm (28,7 x 36,2 in)

**Starlit Rapsody**
Oil on Linen, 2002, 162 x 130 cm (63,8 x 51,2 in)

ART IS THE VISIBLE

ex**P**RESSION

OF THE INVISIBLE WORLD

**Tender Love**
Oil on Linen, 2007, 130 x 162 cm (51,2 x 63,8 in)

THE MEMORY OF THAT LOVE

KEEPS COMING BACK TO ME

REPEATING ITSELF LIKE A REFRAIN

OF THE SONG OF MY SOUL

**Perfect Love**
Oil on Linen, 2007, 162 x 130 cm (63,8 x 51,2 in)

MY PAINTINGS ARE

A MANIFESTATION OF

MY OWN HEART

**Lovers**
Oil on Linen, 2002, 97 x 130 cm (38,2 x 51,2 in)

flOwers

ARE

THE MOST EMOTIVE
AND BEAUTIFUL GIFT
THAT EACH ONE OF US
HAS BEEN GIVEN
ON OUR JOURNEY

**Lilies of April**
Oil on Linen, 2003, 116 x 89 cm (45,7 x 35,1 in)

**Hugs and Kisses**
Oil on Linen, 2001, 92 x 73 cm (36,2 x 28,7 in)

FLOWERS

ARE

GOD'S MESSENGERS

OF LOVE

FLOWERS ARE
GOD'S GIFT TO US
TO MEASURE ALL
THE BEAUTY BY

**Honolulu Wings**
Acrylic on Canvas, 2004, 116 x 89 cm (45,7 x 35,1 in)

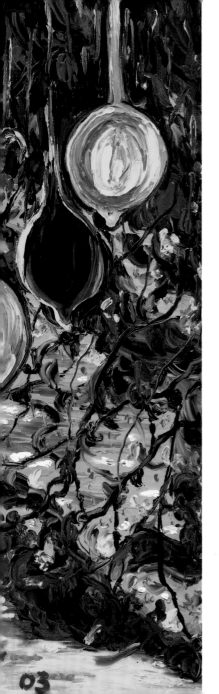

A

GARDEN

IS

PLANTED

# O N E

FLOWER AT A TIME

**African Harvest**
Oil on Linen, 2003, 114 x 146 cm (44,9 x 57,5 in)

HE BROUGHT ME DAISIES IN THE MORNING
SO LIGHT AND FRESH AND WET WITH DEW

I GAVE HIM DAFFODILS AT SUNSET
THAT SCENTED THE RAYS ON THEIR WING

**African Meadow**
Oil on Linen, 2006, 130 x 97 cm (51,2 x 38,2 in)

**Wild Lupins**
Oil on Linen, 2006, 100 x 81 cm (39,4 x 31,9 in)

PAINTING FLOWERS AND UNDERSTANDING

THEM IS UNDERSTANDING LIFE ITSELF

# grAce

## TO ME

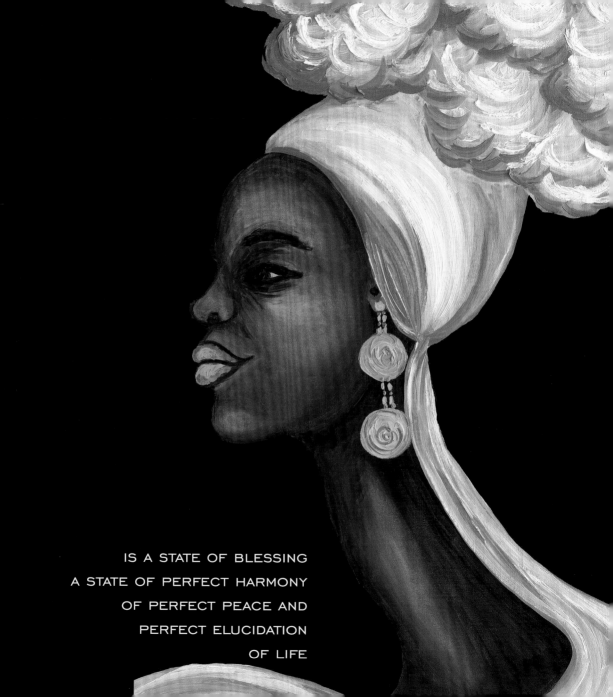

IS A STATE OF BLESSING
A STATE OF PERFECT HARMONY
OF PERFECT PEACE AND
PERFECT ELUCIDATION
OF LIFE

**Zaharat**
Oil on Linen, 1995, 61 x 50 cm (24,1 x 19,7 in)

**Sati of Tumbu**
Oil on Linen, 1995, 61 x 50 cm (24,1 x 19,7 in)

ENDURANCE ALWAYS HAS THE LAST WORD

ART COMES FROM SIMPLICITY, PURITY AND BALANCE CREATES ART

**Little Bird**
Oil on Linen, 1999, 92 x 73 cm (36,2 x 28,7 in)

KNOWING YOURSELF

## IS

THE MOST DIFFICULT KNOWLEDGE TO OBTAIN

**Proud Maya**
Oil on Linen, 2002, 92 x 73 cm (36,2 x 28,7 in)

MY ART IS

THE MIRR O R

OF MY UNIVERSE

OF MY UNIVERSE

THE MIRR O R

MY ART IS

**Lady's Maid**
Oil on Linen, 1998, 130 x 162 cm (51,2 x 63,8 in)

**Contentment**
Oil on Linen, 2003, 89 x 116 cm (35,1 x 45,7 in)

**Rieko**
Oil on Linen, 1998, 65 x 50 cm (25,6 x 19,7 in)

**Birth of Sita**
Oil on Linen, 2007, 195 x 195 cm (76,8 x 76,8 in)

ART IS THE MANIFESTATION OF THE EXPERIENCES OF THE SOUL

**Shinnosuke's Art**
Oil on Linen, 2006, 195 x 195 cm (76,8 x 76,8 in)

FROM A HEALTHY AND DISCIPLINED MIND

COMES THE FLOURISHING OF LIFE

MY ART IS A H**A**NDPRINT

OF MY SOUL

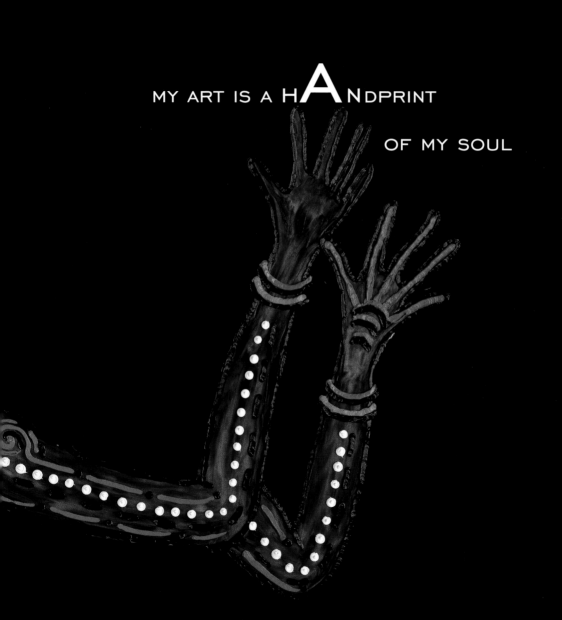

THROUGH IT
I WILL BLESS ALL THOSE
THAT LOOK UPON IT

**Karo Dancer**
Oil on Linen, 2006, 130 x 97 cm (51,2 x 38,2 in)

**High Voodoo**
Oil on Linen, 2007, 195 x 195 cm (76,8 x 76,8 in)

ART IS A SPIRITUAL MANIFESTATION OF THINGS PERCEIVED

**Prince of Dance**
Oil on Linen, 2007, 195 x 195 cm (76,8 x 76,8 in)

Prince with a New Fan
Oil on Linen, 2007, 130 x 97 cm (51,2 x 38,2 in)

DEDICATION AND DISCIPLINE

ARE MOTHER AND FATHER

OF GENIUS

GO **BOLDLY** AND

CREATE THE IMPOSSIBLE

Rose Hanuman
Oil on Linen, 2006, 116 x 89 cm (45,7 x 35,1 in)

A
TRAINED
DISCIPLINED MIND
WITH VERY FEW ACTIONS
CAN SHOW GREAT DEPTH
OF UNDERSTANDING
AND CONVEY THAT TO OUR EYES

**Ganjiro**
Oil on Linen, 2005, 195 x 195 cm (76,8 x 76,8 in)

IF YOU CAN SEE THE COLOUR

OF THE WORLD

IT IS HEAVEN

IT IS A BEAUTIFUL W O RLD

**Inca Artisan**
Oil on Linen, 2004, 97 x 130 cm (38,2 x 51,2 in)

Endless Feeling
Oil on Linen, 2007, 195 x 130 cm (76,8 x 51,2 in)

# THERE IS A TALENT IN EACH ONE OF US

## THE MAGIC IS TO UNLOCK THAT TALENT

TREE, WHO ARE YOU?

YOUR TRUNK IS FAMILIAR.
I RECOGNIZE THE SCABS THAT FORMED
AROUND YOUR GIRTH
TO BRAVE THE WOUNDS OF THE STORMS
THAT WHIPPED YOU.
YOUR GNARLS STILL WEEP
OVER YOUNG BRANCHES CUT TOO SOON
IN SPRING.

YOUR ARMS ARE BENT AND
POINT TO THE EARTH,
WHERE FROZEN SNOW HAS SLID
AFTER THE STRUGGLE.

YOUR ROOTS GROW DEEPER
WITH THE BEATING OF THE SEASONS,
LIKE STRONG ROPES IN SEARCH OF A HAVEN.

YOU BRING OUT YOUR GLORY
IN SHOWERS OF PETALS
AND TELL US THAT IT IS SPRING.

YOU BRING YOUR FRUIT AND OFFER
ALL YOU HAVE TO ANY PASSER BY.

WHO ARE YOU TREE?
WHY DO YOU ACCEPT YOUR DESTINY AND
WELCOME THE BIRDS TO RAISE
THEIR YOUNG IN YOUR ARMS?

YOU OFFER SHADE TO ANY IDLE BEING SO FREELY
AND ASK FOR NOTHING IN RETURN.
NO TOLL — NO PAYMENT — NOT EVEN A PRAYER?

WHO ARE YOU TREE?
HOW MANY ARE YOUR CHILDREN?

WHO CARES FOR YOU?

WHO LOVES **YOU** BACK?

Hawaiian Sunset (detail)
Oil on Linen, 2002, 81 x 65 cm (31,9 x 25,6 in)

Art is a manifestation
of the spiritual forms and ideas,
which the viewer recognizes
as part of his own experience

THROUGH THE BLUSHING PETALS

OF CHERRY BLOSSOM FOR

IN TOTAL SILENCE

THEY ARE BORN AND

IN TOTAL SILENCE

THEY PASS AWAY

**Dance of Spring (1-3)**
Oil on Linen, 2004, 162 x 130 cm (63,8 x 51,2 in)

**Gift of Love**
Oil on Linen, 1999, 92 x 73 cm (36,2 x 28,7 in)

# LIFE GLIDES

IT DOES NOT RUSH

IT IS LIFE

WHICH IS TAKEN

AS A GIFT

**By the Blue Pool**
Oil on Linen, 1998, 130 x 162 cm (51,2 x 63,8 in)

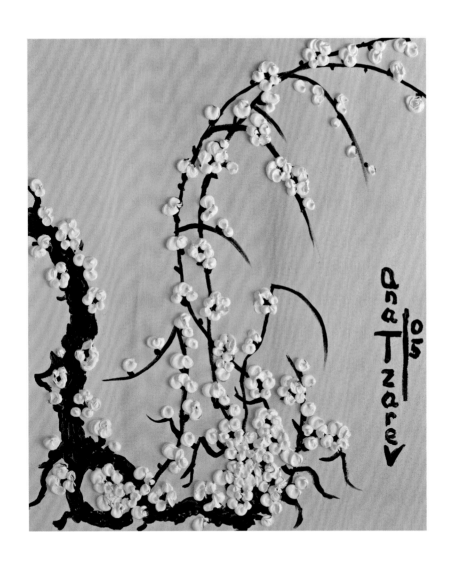

**Michiyo**
Oil on Linen, 2005, 55 x 46 cm (21,7 x 18,1 in)

LIFE GOES ON IN DIFFERENT DIMENSIONS

A SPIRIT IS IN EVERYTHING

EVERY ATOM THAT THIS UNIVERSE POSSESSES

LIFE IS JUST A RAY OF LIGHT

THAT DROPS ONTO THE MOVING WAVE AND

DISAPPEARS INTO THE UNKNOWN

Princess Likelike Welcoming the Spirit of Princess Ka'iulani
Oil on Linen, 2003, 195 x 195 cm (76,8 x 76,8 in)

**Petits Bonshommes Musiciens**
Oil on Linen, 2002, 195 x 195 cm (76,8 x 76,8 in)

MY ART IS A CREATIVE LIFE DANCE OF SEARCH,

RECOGNITION AND AFFIRMATION OF ALL LIFE

# PAINTING

IS

MYSTERY

**Heron Maiden**
Oil on Linen, 2005, 195 x 195 cm (76,8 x 76,8 in)

## SOLITUDE

IS THE BIRTH
OF FOCUS

**Enlightenment**
Oil on Linen, 2003, 65 x 81 cm (25,6 x 31,9 in)

IN SILENT SANCTUARY

**WISDOM** IS BORN

**Old Inca Chief**
Oil on Linen, 2003, 92 x 73 cm (36,2 x 28,7 in)

SPIRITUALITY EXPANDS
WITH UNDERSTANDING
THE PATH OF EVOLUTION

# OF ALL THINGS

Ana Tzarev in Varanasi, India 2007

A PRAYER

FOR THE WORLD

WITH EVERY TURN

OF THE WHEEL

**Large Buddhist Prayer Wheels**
Oil on Linen, 2003, 130 x 97 cm (51,2 x 38,2 in)

**Honi**
Oil on Linen, 2003, 90 x 92 cm (35,4 x 36,2 in)

ART IS A MANIFESTATION OF THINGS PERCEIVED IN SPIRIT

# KNOWLEDGE

IS THE ONLY RICHNESS

WORTH STRIVING FOR

**Winter Days**
Oil on Linen, 2002, 81 x 65 cm (31,9 x 25,6 in)

**Light**
Oil on Linen, 1998, 54 x 73 cm (21,3 x 28,7 in)

ART IS A LGHTHOUSE

TO FUTURE GENERATIONS

PAINTING GIVES **W**INGS TO MY SOUL
AND LIFTS ME INTO A REALM OF PURE,
DEEP, SPIRITUAL UNION WITH THE INFINITE,
WHERE ALL THE SENSE OF TIME IS LOST

**African Butterflies**
Oil on Linen, 2003, 100 x 81 cm (39,4 x 31,9 in)

# OUT OF

DEVASTATION

BIRTH

COMES                    OF NEW LIFE

**Mother's Grief**
Oil on Linen, 2004, 100 x 81 cm (39,4 x 31,9 in)

Friendship
Oil on Linen, 2001, 73 x 92 cm (28,7 x 36,2 in)

THE DISPOSSESSED

MOVE MY SOUL

MY BRUSH RECORDS

THAT FEELING

I WILL STAND MY WATCH

OVER THE **PEOPLE**

WITH BARBED WIRE HEARTS

Displaced
Oil on Linen, 2001, 92 x 73 cm (36,2 x 28,7 in)

**The Summit**
Oil on Linen, 1999, 73 x 92 cm (28,7 x 36,2 in)

# LONELINESS IS

A LACK OF APPRECIATION

OF THE NEEDS

OF OTHER PEOPLE

**L**ACK OF RESOURCES
CREATES POVERTY BUT
IT IS THE LACK OF KNOWLEDGE
THAT SUSTAINS IT

**Seven Sisters**
Oil on Linen, 2004, 130 x 195 cm (51,2 x 76,8 in)

# EDUCATION

BRINGS WISDOM AND PROSPERITY

IT IS THE **PROSPERITY** THAT IS

THE MOTHER OF WORLD **PEACE**

**Evening in the Tent**
Oil on Linen, 2001, 81 x 100 cm (31,9 x 39,4 in)

**Killing Fields**
Oil on Linen, 2001, 130 x 195 cm (51,2 x 76,8 in)

A HEROIN POPPY

IS TO ME A COBRA

A SNAke LOOKING AT ME

WITH HOPE

WE PROGRESS

IT IS A WORD

THAT LEADS US

TO THE

FUTURE

**After the Storm**
Oil on Linen, 2001, 140 x 146 cm (55,1 x 57,5 in)

ENCOURAGEMENT IS

THE BEAUTIFUL GIFT OF ENERGY

THAT GIVES IMPETUS AND HOPE

# TO ACHIEVE THE GREAT DREAM

Colours of the Orient
Oil on Linen, 2000, 162 x 130 cm (63,8 x 51,2 in)

**Big Beauty**
Oil on Linen, 1996, 97 x 130 cm (38,2 x 51,2 in)

HAVE THE COURAGE AND
TAKE JUST ONE STEP AND
YOU WILL DISCOVER THAT
THE WHOLE JOURNEY IS —
JUST THAT ONE STEP —
TAKEN AT A TIME

Ana Tzarev, Mali 2006

HOPE

GIVES US AN INCENTIVE

FOR THE FUTURE

TOMORROW IS

ALWAYS FULL OF

# HOPE

**Long Walk**
Oil on Linen, 1996, 97 x 130 cm (38,2 x 51,2 in)

AN EMPTY PLACE

IS A CRADLE

OF UNTOLD

POSSIBILITIES

**Little Helper**
Oil on Linen, 2001, 73 x 92 cm (28,7 x 36,2 in)

**Red Sunset**
Oil on Linen, 2000, 114 x 146 cm (44,9 x 57,5 in)

**Spring Ritual**
Oil on Linen, 2001, 36 x 46 cm (14,1 x 18,1 in)

AS I TRAVEL THROUGH TIME
I RECORD MY EXPERIENCES IN PAINTINGS
AND LEAVE THEM AS POSTCARDS

TO

FUTURE

GENERATIONS

# INDEX

*Tender Love* (detail)

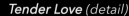

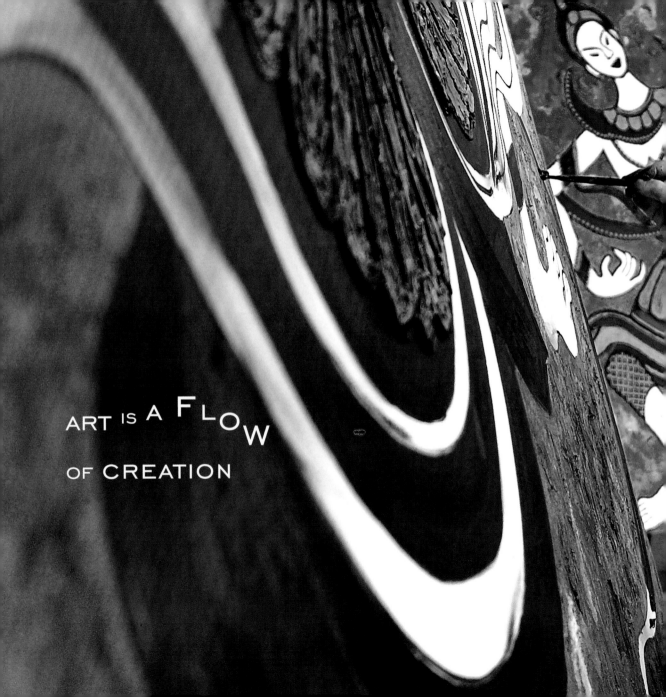

ART IS A FLOW
OF CREATION

WHEN SOMETHING PER

AS IMAGINED IS BORN

IT IS A MANIFESTATION

OF THE INNER SPIRITU

AND FEELINGS OF THE

ONE USES

NG CANDLE

HT OTHER CANDLES

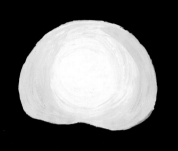

SO THE WORK OF ART

LIGHTS A FLAME OF INSPIRATION

IN ANOTHER HUMAN BEING

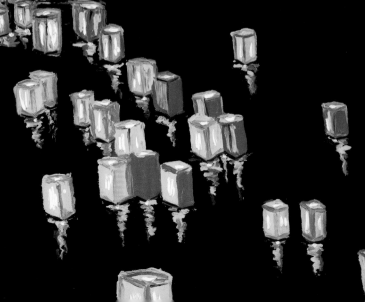

OnaTzarev